Living vs. Nonliving

by Maddie Spalding

The Child's World®
childsworld.com

Published by The Child's World®
1980 Lookout Drive • Mankato, MN 56003-1705
800-599-READ • www.childsworld.com

Photographs ©: James Steidl/Shutterstock
Images, cover, 1; Shutterstock Images, 5, 18,
21; Zeljko Radojko/Shutterstock Images, 6;
Romolo Tavani/Shutterstock Images, 9; Diane
Diederich/Shutterstock Images, 11; Nicolas
Primola/Shutterstock Images, 13; David T. Clay/
Shutterstock Images, 14; iStockphoto, 17

ISBN 9781503844445 (Reinforced Library Binding)
ISBN 9781503846623 (Portable Document Format)
ISBN 9781503847811 (Online Multi-user eBook)
LCCN 2019956594

Printed in the United States of America

JUVNONFIC
510 SPA

About the Author

Maddie Spalding is a writer
and editor. She lives in
Minneapolis, Minnesota.
She enjoys reading and
hiking in her spare time.

TABLE of CONTENTS

CHAPTER ONE
Living and Nonliving Things . . . 4

CHAPTER TWO
Features of Living Things . . . 8

CHAPTER THREE
Features of Nonliving Things . . . 16

Living vs. Nonliving Chart . . . 22

Glossary . . . 23

To Learn More . . . 24

Index . . . 24

Living and Nonliving Things

It is a warm fall day. Josh and his family are on a hike. They walk along a stream. Brown leaves crunch under their feet. Josh sits on a boulder to catch his breath. He sees something small running across the path. It is a lizard!

The sun is starting to sink lower in the sky. Josh hears a bird singing nearby. The sound comes from a robin. It sits on a branch high up in a tree. The woods around him seem full of life. Some things that Josh sees are living. But some are nonliving. Living and nonliving things are everywhere.

Lizards are living.
Rocks are nonliving.

Some nonliving things, such as fallen leaves, were once living.

Scientists **classify** things to better understand them. Living and nonliving are categories. Living things have certain features. For example, they grow and take in food. Lizards and birds are living things. So are trees and people.

Other things do not have these features. They are not alive. Water, rocks, and the sun are nonliving things. Things that die also become nonliving. Some trees shed their leaves in fall. Fallen leaves are nonliving. They were once part of a living thing. They grew on trees. But they died after they fell from the trees. They stopped growing.

CHAPTER TWO

Features of Living Things

Living things are also called **organisms**. They have special qualities. These features describe what the organism can do. If something has all these features, it is living.

Cells are the building blocks of living things. All living things are made of cells. The human body has trillions of cells. Different parts of the body are made of different kinds of cells.

Living things can move on their own. Sometimes this movement is obvious. It is easy to tell when someone is walking or running. But some organisms move slowly. Their movements are less obvious. For example, plants move slowly. They follow where the sun is in the sky.

Plants can move
toward sunlight.

9

Plants bend toward sunlight. They do this to get as much sunlight as possible. They need sunlight to grow.

All living things breathe. Most breathe in oxygen. Then they breathe out carbon dioxide. This process is called respiration. Plants take in carbon dioxide. They release oxygen.

Living things also eat or take in food. Some make their own food. Plants make food from sunlight. Light is **energy**. Plants capture this energy. Plant cells turn this energy into sugar. The sugar is plant food. This process is called photosynthesis. Food contains **nutrients**. Nutrients help living things grow and function. Living things also need water.

Other organisms cannot make their own food. They eat other organisms. For example, people eat plants such as vegetables. Many people also eat animals. They get their nutrients from these organisms.

Living things break down food to get energy. This process is called digestion. Living things do not need all of the nutrients they take in. The extra materials are waste. Living things get rid of waste.

Animals eat food because they cannot make their own.

Living things can **reproduce**. Some lay eggs. Others give birth to live **offspring**. Still others reproduce in different ways. Bacteria have only one cell. They divide to reproduce. Flowers reproduce from pollen. Pollen is a grain that flowers make. Insects, bats, and birds feed on flowers. They carry pollen from one flower to another. The wind can blow pollen to another flower. Then the second flower uses the pollen to make seeds. An animal or the wind scatters the seeds. The seeds grow into new plants.

All living things grow. Energy from food helps them grow. The organisms make new cells. Then they get bigger. People and many animals are born small. They grow over time. Some organisms change shape. Butterflies hatch from eggs as caterpillars. A caterpillar makes a protective covering. This is a **chrysalis**. The caterpillar grows wings while inside the chrysalis. It leaves the chrysalis when it is grown. Then it is a butterfly.

BUTTERFLY LIFE CYCLE

Adult

Eggs

Caterpillar

Chrysalis

13

All living things have a life cycle. Some caterpillars change into butterflies as part of their life cycle.

The changes living things go through are part of its life cycle. An organism's life cycle is everything that happens from birth to death. All living things are born. They grow and get bigger. Many reproduce. They later die. The life cycle continues with their offspring. Their offspring go through these changes, too.

Living things can also sense changes in their environments. They can tell what is going on around them. They use their senses. Some have only a few senses. For example, earthworms do not have eyes or ears. They rely on their sense of touch. Other animals have many senses. They can touch, taste, and smell things. They can also see and hear things. They can sense food nearby. They can also sense danger. Animals may see or hear a **predator**. They may also smell the predator. They respond to this change in their environment. They may run or hide. Or they may defend themselves.

Features of Nonliving Things

Nonliving things are not alive. They do not have the features of living things. Some were never alive. They do not have cells. Others were once alive. They became nonliving when they died. The cells of the organism are still there. But they no longer work. The organism no longer breathes or shows signs of life.

Fossils are nonliving things. But the creatures they show were once alive thousands or millions of years ago.

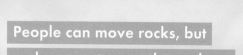

People can move rocks, but
rocks cannot move themselves.

Nonliving things do not breathe. They also do not eat. They do not need nutrients. Nutrients give living things energy. But nonliving things do not move by themselves. So they do not need energy. People can move nonliving things. For example, people can lift rocks. But rocks cannot move by themselves.

Nonliving things also do not reproduce. Many already exist in the world. Other nonliving things are made. People make many objects. For example, they make cars. Cars are nonliving things.

Nonliving things can grow. But they grow in a different way than organisms do. They grow when more of the same material is added. Rain and floods add more water to lakes. The water makes the lakes bigger.

Organisms depend on nonliving things. They need water and oxygen to survive. Dead things also help feed living things. Many living animals eat dead animals. Dead things also **decompose**. They break down. Worms and other organisms eat them. These organisms live in soil. Parts of the dead things remain in the soil. They become plant food. They are nutrients. They help plants grow.

Crystals are nonliving. But they grow bigger when more material is added.

Living vs. Nonliving

Can move on their own	Cannot move on their own
Can sense changes in their environment	Cannot sense changes in their environment
Grow and develop	Some can get bigger if more of the same material is added
Are made up of cells	Those that were never living don't have cells. Dead things have cells, but the cells no longer work.

Glossary

chrysalis (KRIS-uh-lis) A chrysalis is a hard shell that protects a caterpillar as it turns into a butterfly. The chrysalis was attached to a tree.

classify (KLASS-ih-fye) To classify is to put things into groups based on their qualities or characteristics. Scientists classify things as living or nonliving.

decompose (dee-kuhm-POZE) To decompose is to rot and break down. Dead things decompose.

energy (EN-ur-jee) Energy is a measure of something's ability to do work or create change. Living things get energy from food.

nutrients (NOO-tree-entz) Nutrients are substances that organisms need to live and grow. Food contains nutrients.

offspring (AHF-spring) Offspring are an animal's babies. Some animals give birth to live offspring while others lay eggs.

organisms (OR-gan-iz-umz) Organisms are living things. Plants and animals are types of organisms.

predator (PRED-uh-tur) A predator is an animal that hunts and eats other animals. Living things can sense when a predator is nearby.

reproduce (ree-proh-DEWSS) To reproduce is to have young. Living things can reproduce.

To Learn More

In the Library

Kurtz, Kevin. *Living Things and Nonliving Things: A Compare and Contrast Book*. Mt. Pleasant, SC: Arbordale Publishing, 2017.

Rice, William B. *Ecosystems*. Huntington Beach, CA: Teacher Created Materials, 2015.

Spalding, Maddie. *The Animal Life Cycle*. Mankato, MN: The Child's World, 2019.

On the Web

Visit our website for links about living and nonliving things:
childsworld.com/links

Note to Parents, Teachers, and Librarians: We routinely verify our Web links to make sure they are safe and active sites. So encourage your readers to check them out!

Index

breathing, 10, 16–19
cells, 8–10, 12, 16
decompose, 20

food, 7, 10–12, 15, 20
growth, 7, 10, 12–15, 20

life cycle, 13, 15
organisms, 8, 11–15, 16, 20

reproduce, 12–15, 19
senses, 15